ADJUSTMENTS FOR FINANCIAL STATEMENTS

ADJUSTMENTS FOR ACCOUNTS

Toye Adelaja

I0476981

INTRODUCTION

In this book, you will learn various ways of making necessary adjustments for financial statements.

You will learn how to record and post correct accounting data and figures in order to generate reliable accounting information which can be used by users of accounting information for informed decision making.

TABLE OF CONTENTS

Chapter 1

CAPITAL EXPENDITURE AND REVENUE EXPENDITURE

Capital expenditure and revenue expenditure have been a source of confusion to many students and business owners. It is necessary to distinguish between the two vividly.

1.1. Capital expenditure

Firstly, you need to understand that capital expenditure is totally different from capital which is the fund contributed by the owner of the business. Capital expenditure is different from capital (owner's equity). Capital is the fund invested in the business by the owner of the business.

Capital expenditure is incurred during the course of the business to acquire non-current assets or to increase the value of existing non-current assets. Capital expenditure does not appear in a statement of comprehensive income (profit and loss accounts). It appears in a statement of financial position (balance sheet) alone. Examples of capital expenditures are:

1) Acquisition of non- current assets
2) Cost of bringing the assets into the business premises
3) Installation cost of the non-current assets
4) Legal cost of buying buildings
5) Cost of putting the non-current assets into use.
6) Import duty paid on importing non-current assets

1.2. Revenue expenditure

Revenue expenditure can be defined as routine expenditure of a business. This type of expenditure is necessary for the maintenance of earnings capacity, upkeep of the fixed assets in a fully efficient state, and the total cash spent in normal selling including the cost of goods and services of the business. It is not the cost incurred on acquisition of non- current assets or cost of increasing the value of non- current assets.

Differences between capital expenditure and revenue expenditure can be explained further by the table below:

Details of Expenditures	Types of Expenditures
Fuel cost	Revenue
Expansion of business premises	Capital
Cost of renovating office	Revenue
Buying vehicle	Capital
Repair of vehicle	Revenue
Electricity cost	Revenue
Replacing parts of machinery	Revenue
Increasing capacity of machinery	Capital

It has already been mentioned that capital expenditure should be treated in a statement of financial position, and revenue expenditure should be treated in the statement of comprehensive income. Efforts should be made not to intermingle the posting of the above mentioned transactions in the books of account in order to avoid costly errors. If there are joint expenditures that combine both capital expenditures and revenue expenditures, the expenditures need to be separated before posting.

1. 3. Capital receipts

Sale of an item of capital expenditure is classified as capital receipt. For example, machinery that costs $15,000 was sold for $1,500 after 4years. $15,000 was treated as capital expenditure, while $1,500 received is treated as capital receipt and credited to machinery disposal account in the general ledger account.

1.4. Revenue receipts

Revenue receipts are all the revenue, and other income such as discount received and commissions receivable that are added to gross profit to get total income.

ILLUSTRATION 1

Mr. Femi, a farmer bought a tractor and 10 cutlasses for $450,000 and $850 respectively. He incurred the following expenses for the year ended 31st December, 2012.

Wages	$69,000
Yam tuba	$11,000
Maize	$2,000

He received $4,900 from customers. The tractor was later sold for $250,000. Compute the following:

a) Capital Expenditure

b) Revenue Expenditure

c) Revenue Receipts

d) Capital Receipts

Solution

a) Capital Expenditure

	$
Tractor	450,000
Cutlasses	850
Capital Expenditure	450,850

b) Revenue Expenditure

	$
Wages	69,000
Yam tuba	11,000
Maize	2,000
Revenue Expenditure	82,000

c) Revenue Receipts

Amount received from customers is his revenue receipts.

Revenue Receipts = $4,900

d) Capital Receipts

The amount at which the tractor was sold is his capital receipts.

Capital Receipts = $250,000

1.5. Multi-choice Questions

Choose the correct answers from the following questions:

1. Which of the following is a revenue receipt?
   A. Revaluation of assets
   B. Sales proceeds of a motor vehicle
   C. Sales of finished goods
   D. Income from sales of shares

2. Which of the following is not a capital expenditure?
   A. Extension of office building
   B. Acquisition of machinery
   C. Purchase of computer for resale
   D. Purchase of Motor Vehicle

3. An example of capital gain

A. Share premium

B. Share discount

C. Bonus issue

D. dividend

Solution:
   1. C
   2. C
   3. A

Chapter 2

BAD DEBTS AND ALLOWANCES FOR DOUBTFUL DEBTS

2.1. Bad debts

Credit sales cannot be totally eradicated in a business. It forms large amount of sales made by many companies. There is a probability that some of the customers may not pay for the goods purchased on credit. The business entity therefore, suffers the risk of default.

The default is called bad debts in accounting. It is classified as a normal business expense. It should be charged to an income statement as an expense for the period. It should also be deducted from asset accounts (**Account Receivable**).

To record a bad debt; debit it to bad debt account so as to increase expense account, and credit it to debtors' account to reduce the debt or eradicate the debt.

There are different probable circumstances that may exist concerning a bad debt. They are as follows:

> 1) The debtors died or go bankrupt; it is inevitable that nothing can be received.
>
> 2) The debtor indicates that only part of the total amount due on the invoice will be paid by him.

The above two statements can be illustrated **in the book of Smith Ltd** below:

1) The debtors (T.Jev) died or go bankrupt; it is inevitable that nothing can be received.

T. Jev
Accounts

2010		$	2010		$
			Dec.	Bad	
March 1	Sales	400	31	debt	400

2) The debtor (B. Blazer) indicates that only part of the total amount due on the invoice will be paid by him.

B. Blazer Accounts

2010		$	2010		$
			Sept.		
Jan. 3	Sales	500	18	Bank	350
				Bad	
			Dec.31	debt	150
		500			500

Bad debts

2010		$	2010		$
			Dec.		
Dec.31	T. Jev	400	31	P&L	550
Dec.31	B.Blazer	150			
		550			550

An extract of income statement (P&L) for the year ended 31 December 2010.

	$
Gross Profit	XX
Less Expenses	
Bad debts	(550)

Note: It is assumed that the above transactions are recorded in a book of a particular business; let say in the book of Smith Ltd.

2.2. Allowances for Doubtful Debts

Death and bankruptcy may make it impossible for debtors to pay their debts. It means that the amounts owed by debtors become irrecoverable and shall be treated as a trading loss for the period under consideration.

In a situation where the deceased customer leaves an estate, the estate shall contribute to the recovery of the debts. The difference between the total debts owed by the deceased debtor and the amount the estate is able to contribute shall be considered as bad debts.

The main aim of allowance for doubtful debts is to record accounts receivable in the statement of financial position at a realistic value. The estimation of how probable and likely a debt will be bad is called allowance for doubtful debt or provision for doubtful debt.

It is difficult to determine with certainty at the end of a month or a year the true amount of debt that will not be paid by debtors. How do you decide on the allowance? For the purpose of arriving at a figure for allowance for doubtful debt, a business entity must first consider that some debtors will not pay any of their debts, while some will pay a portion of the amount owing only, leaving the remainder permanently unpaid.

The estimate figure can be determined in the following ways:

1. by looking at individual debt, and deciding to what extent it will be bad;
2. by estimating on the basis of past experience, what percentage of the total debts remaining unpaid will finally prove to be bad debts.

It is generally believed that the longer a debt is being owed, the more likely it is going to be bad debt.
Some business entities prepare an "ageing schedule" showing how long a debt has been remained unpaid.

Older debtors should be assigned higher percentage estimate than newer debtors.

DEBTORS AGEING SCHEDULE

Period of debt	Amount	Estimate percentage of doubtful debts	Allowance for doubtful debts
	$	%	
Less than 1 Month	2,500	2	50
1 Month to 3 months	1,500	4	60
3 months to 6 months	400	5	20
6 months to 1 year	100	6	6
over 1 year	80	15	12
Total	4,580		148

Allowance for doubtful debt should be debited to an income statement. Here is an example:

An extract of income statement (P&L) for the year ended 31 December, 2010.

	$
Gross Profit	XX
Less Expenses:	
Bad debts	-550
Allowances for doubtful debt	-60

2.2.1. Increase in Allowance for Doubtful Debts

When the total accounts receivable in a current year increases more than the previous year, each of the accounts receivable for the previous year (opening balance) and the account receivable for the current year (closing balance) should be multiplied by the rate of allowance for doubtful debts to get allowance for doubtful debts for each year. The difference between the two results (closing allowance for doubtful debts minus opening allowance for doubtful debts) should be charged (debited) to a statement of comprehensive income (Profit and Loss Accounts) if the result is positive. The amount reduces profit.

The closing balance of the accounts receivable should be multiplied by a rate of allowance for doubtful debt, and posted to a statement of financial position as a deduction from the accounts receivable for the current year. The following illustration can be used to explain it further.

ILLUSTRATION 1

The following were extracted from the books of Jando as at 31st Dec. 2013.
Accounts receivable brought forward from the previous year is $20,000. Accounts receivable for the current year is $24,000. You are given that the rate of allowance for doubtful debts is 2%. You are required to record the above transactions in the books of accounts of Jando.

Solution:

1) Debit profit and loss account with ($24,000-$20,000)2%
2) Credit allowance for doubtful debt accounts with $80

Allowance for Doubtful Debts Accounts

2013		$	2013		$
			Jan. 1	Balance b/f	400
Dec. 31	Balance	480		P & L	80
		480			480
			Jan.1 2014	Balance b/d	480

Profit and Loss Accounts

2013	$	2013	$
Allowance for doubtful debts	80		

Statement of Comprehensive income for the year eneded 31st Dec. 2013

Gross Profit	XX
Less allowance for doubtful debts (increase)	-80

Statement of financial position as at 31st December, 2013

	$	$
Current Assets:		
Accounts receivable	24,000	
Less: allowance for doubtful debt	-480	
	23,520	

NOTE:

2% is the rate of allowance for doubtful debt. It should be used to multiply account receivable for each period to get the allowance for doubtful debt for each period.

The increase in the value of allowance for doubtful debt ($80) is debited (deducted from the income) to statement of comprehensive income.

The closing balance of allowance for doubtful debts ($480) is deducted from accounts receivable to get the realistic value of accounts receivable.

2. 2. 2. Decrease in Allowance for Doubtful Debts

You need to do the opposite of what you did to the increase in allowance for doubtful debt, in order to decrease the allowance.

Where the accounts receivable in a current year is less than that of previous year, the allowance for doubtful debt in the current year will be less than the allowance for doubtful debt in the previous year and hence, the profit and loss account should be credited with the difference between the two allowances for doubtful debts.

Double entry bookkeeping for the records are:

    1) Debit Allowance for Doubtful Debts Accounts

2) Credit Profit and Loss Accounts

ILLUSTRATION 2

The following were extracted from the books of Smith Ltd as at 31St Dec. 2012.

Accounts receivable brought forward is $20,000. Accounts receivable as at 31St Dec.2012 is $17,000. You are given that the rate of allowance for doubtful debt is 2%. You are required to prepare the necessary accounts.

SOLUTION

Allowance for doubtful debts

2012		$	2012		$
	P & L	60	Jan. 1	Balance b/f	400
Dec. 31	Balance	340			
		400			400
			2013		
			Jan. 1	Balance b/d	340

Profit and Loss Accounts				
2012		$	2012	$
			Allowance for doubtful Debts	60

Statement of Comprehensive income for the year ended 31st Dec.2012

	$
Gross Profit	XX
Add allowance for doubtful debts (decrease)	60

Statement of financial position as at 31st December, 2012

	$
Current Asset:	
Account receivable	17,000
Less: allowance for doubtful debts	-340
	16,660

ILLUSTRATION 3

Year to 31st Dec.	Debtors after bad debts written off $	Allowance for doubtful debts $
1990	60,000	600
1991	65,000	650
1992	63,000	630

a) What was the treatment of allowance for doubtful debts in the statement of comprehensive income (Profit and Loss Account) for 1991?

b) In 1992, debtors figure will appear in the statement of financial position (balance sheet) as

SOLUTION:

a) $50 should be debited to a statement of comprehensive income.

b) $63,000 – $630 = $62,370

ILLUSTRATION 4

The accounts receivable of a trading concern is $66,000. Out of this, 2% is irrecoverable;
5 percent of the balance is unlikely to be collected.

a) How much is the bad debt?

b) What is the allowance for doubtful debt?

Solution:

a. 66,000 × 2% = $1,320

b. (66,000 -1,320)×5% = $3,234

ILLUSTRATION 5

Use the following information to answer questions a. & b.
Accounts Receivables as at   1/6/2013 $300,450
Accounts Receivables as at   31/5/2014 $525,110
Specific bad debts during the year $41,000
Allowance for bad and doubtful debts as at 1/6/2013 $12,500
The provision for bad and doubtful debts is maintained at a level of 5% of accounts receivables as at 31/5/2014.

a. What is the value of Accounts Receivables as at 31/5/2014 to be shown in the statement of financial position (balance sheet)?

b. What is the amount of allowance for bad and doubtful debts to be recorded in statement of comprehensive income (profit and loss accounts) for the year ended 31 May 2014?

SOLUTION:

a. Account Receivable to be shown in the statement of financial position

	$
Accounts receivable 31/5/2014	525,110
Less Bad debt for the year	(41,000)
	484,110
Allowance for doubtful debts(484,110×5%)	(24,206)
	459,904

The value of Accounts Receivables as at 31/5/2014 to be shown in the statement of financial position (balance sheet) is $459,904.

b. Allowance for bad and doubtful debts to be shown in the statements of comprehensive income (profit and loss accounts)

Allowance for bad and doubtful debts Accounts

	$		$
		Balance b/d	12,500
Balance c/d	24,206	Income(P&L)	11,706
	24,206		24,206
		Balance b/d	24,206

The amount of allowance for bad and doubtful debts to be recorded (debited) in the statement of comprehensive income (profit and loss accounts) for the year ended 31 May 2014 is $11,706.

2.3. Bad Debts Recovered

Sometimes, a debt written off in previous years may be recovered.

The accounting entries for the above statement are:

1. return the debt by making the following entries:

Dr: Debtor's account

Cr: Bad debts recovered account

2. When payment is recovered from the debtor in settlement of all or part of the debt:

Dr: Cash/bank

Cr: Debtor's account

With the amount received.

At the end of the financial year, the credit balance in the bad debts recovered account is transferred either to the bad debts account or direct to the credit side of the profit and loss account at the end of the financial year.

Chapter 3

PREPAID EXPENSES AND ACCRUED EXPENSES

3.1. Prepaid Expenses

Prepaid expenses are the payment paid for services not yet enjoyed. They are also the expenditures that have not been consumed at the end of an accounting period. They constitute costs of future income. Only the portions of the costs actually consumed during an accounting period should be considered as an expense of that period. The amount representing unconsumed costs should be carried forward to the next accounting period. The prepaid expenses should be recorded in the statement of financial position under current asset at the end of an accounting period.

For example, a Landlord collects $100 monthly from his tenant, at the end of the year, the tenant is expected to pay ($100 ×12) = $1,200 to his landlord as rent. But if the tenant paid $2,000, he has overpaid by $800. This $800 is the prepaid rent which is a current asset in the statement of financial position for the period. It is only $1,200 expected to be paid for the year that will appear in the statement of comprehensive income (profit and loss account) of the accounting period. In the future, the total rent he will pay the landlord will be less than $800.

Example 2

A landlord collects $250 monthly from his tenant and the tenant has overpaid $400 in the previous year and during the year, he paid $3,200.

What is the amount that will be considered in the statement of comprehensive income as an expense for the year and the amount that will be shown as a current asset in the statement of financial position as at the year end.

Solution:

	Rent A/C		
	$		$
Balance b/f	400	P&L	3,000
		Balance	
Cash	3,200	c/d	600
	3,600		3,600

The amount that will be recorded in the statement of comprehensive income as an expense for the year is $3,000 and the amount that will be shown as a current asset in the statement of financial position as at the year end is $600.

NOTE:

Prepaid expenses are the opposite of prepaid income.

3.2. Accrual or Accrued Expenses

Accrued expenses are the services enjoyed in the past but payment is yet to be paid. Accrued expenses can also be defined as expenses due but not yet paid for. The portion of the expenses remaining unpaid is called expenses owing or accrual.

Example 1

If wages of workers of a company are $2,000 per annum and $1,800 were settled out of it. The amount owing the workers is $200. The $200 will be posted to statement of financial position as a current liability.

NOTE: Accrued expenses are the opposite of accrued income.

ILLUSTRATION

The illustration below consists of both prepaid and accrued expenses.

The trial balance extracted from the books of Mr. Timi at December 31, 2006 included the following debit balances.

	$
Rent paid	2,000
Rates	1,500
Wages	72,500
Interest on loan	350

The following adjustments have to be made before the preparation of final accounts:

	31/12/2005	31/12/2006
	$	$

Rent outstanding	1,000	500
Rates paid in advance	500	600
Wages accrued	1,000	750
Interest on loan unpaid	1,200	1,400

(a) Show the amount of rates that will be debited to the statement of comprehensive Income (profit and loss accounts) for the year ended 31st December, 2006.

(b) What is the amount of rent that will be debited to profit and loss account for the year ended 31st Dec. 2006?

(c) What is the amount of interest on loan that will be recorded in the statement of financial position (balance sheet) and as what as at 31st Dec. 2006?

(d) Show amount of wages that will appear on the statement of comprehensive income and statement of financial position respectively.

Solution:

(a)

Rates Accounts

	$		$
Balance b/d	500	P&L	1,400
Cash	1,500	Balance c/d	600

		2,000		2,000
Balance b/d		600		

The amount of rates that will be debited to the statement of comprehensive Income (profit and loss accounts) for the year ended 31st December, 2006 is $1,400.

(b)

Rent Accounts

	$		$
Cash	2,000	Balance b/d	1,000
Balance c/d	500	P&L	1,500
	2,500		2,500
		Balance c/d	500

The amount of rent that will be debited to profit and loss account for the year ended 31st Dec. 2006 is $1,500.

(c)

Interest on Loan Accounts

	$		$
Cash	350	Balance b/d	1,200
Balance c/d	1,400	P&L	550
	1,750		1,750
		Balance b/d	1,400

The amount of interest on loan that will be recorded in the statement of financial position (balance sheet) as 31st Dec. 2006 is $1,400 and as current liability.

(d)

Wages Accounts

	$		$
Cash	72,500	Balance b/d	1,000
Balance c/d	750	P&L	72,250
	73,250		73,250
		Balance b/d	750

The amount of wages that will appear on the statement of comprehensive income is $72,250 and statement of financial position is $750.

CHAPTER 4

DEPRECIATION OF NON-CURRENT ASSETS

4.1 **Depreciation**

Depreciation is the part of a non-current asset that is consumed during its period of use by the business.

IAS 16 describes depreciation as,

"Both the decline in value of an asset over time as well as the systematic allocation of the depreciable amount of an asset over its useful life"

Depreciation is an expense. It needs to be charged to the statement of comprehensive income (Profit and Loss account) as an expense. The amount charged in a year for depreciation will be determined based on the amount of economic usefulness of the asset that is put to use.

Total depreciation over the life of a non-current asset can be calculated simply as cost less the amount receivable when the non-current asset is put out of use by a business entity. This amount receivable is commonly referred to as scrap value or residual value of the asset.

Residual value can be determined based on the current market prices of the asset as at the day of the financial position, and not at the day of original purchase of the asset.

Where a non-current asset is sold within the same accounting period at a price lower than its cost of acquisition, the difference should be charged to the income statement as a provision for depreciation for the period. For example, a non-current asset that was bought for $950, was sold for $450 in the same accounting year. The depreciation to be charged to an income statement for the year will be $950 – 450 =$500

Where a non-current asset is used for more than one accounting period, depreciation should be charged for each accounting period. How then do you allocate depreciation to each accounting period? There are many methods for the calculation and allocation of depreciation. The methods may not give the same result. It is important that the depreciation should be shared over the useful life of each asset.

Non-current assets held for sale

Where non-current assets are regrouped as being non-current assets held for sales, depreciation must not be provided for the assets.

4.2. Causes of Depreciation

Reduction in the value of tangible non-current assets can arise as a result of physical deterioration, economic factors, time and depletion. The following are the causes of depreciation:

Physical deterioration

a) Wear and Tear: When non-current assets such as plant and machinery, fixtures and fittings are being used, they will eventually wear out.

b) Rust, erosion, decay and rot: metal in machinery will rust away. Wood rots.

Economic Factors

These may be the causes of an asset not to be put to use despite the fact that the asset is still in good condition and quality. Economic factors can occur in different ways, such as obsolescence and inadequacy.

1) Obsolescence: It occurs when an asset is out of date as a result of advancement in technology.

2) Inadequacy: This occurs when an asset is abandoned as a result of its inability to cope with the expansion and growth of the business. This does not mean that the asset is no longer in good condition. For example, a small grinding machine used for producing animal feeds will be inadequate if the business of the animal feeds becomes very big.

Depletion

Some assets are of wasting nature, probably due to extraction of mineral resources or raw materials from them. Assets such as oil well and quarries come under this heading. Provision for the consumption of an asset of wasting nature is called provision for depletion.

Reason for Charging Depreciation

1. To know the actual net profit for the period
2. To comply with the matching concepts
3. To know the realistic value of the assets on the statements of financial position
4. To provide funds for assets replacement

4.3 Methods of calculating depreciation charges

There are many methods of calculating depreciation. Some of them are stated below:

1. Straight-line method
2. Diminishing or reducing balance method
3. Sum of the years' digit method
4. Annuity system

5. Sinking fund method
6. Insurance policy system
7. Revaluation method
8. Production unit method
9. Machine Hours method
10. Depreciation fund method

4.3.1 How to Calculate Depreciation of Non-Current Asset Based on IFRS

"The depreciation method should reflect the pattern in which the asset's future economic benefits are expected to be consumed by the entity and that appropriateness of the method should be reviewed at least annually in case there has been a change in the expected pattern."

Beyond that, the standard leaves the choice of method to the entity, even though it does cite 'straight-line', 'diminishing balance', and 'units of production' methods.

There are many methods in use for the calculation of depreciation. International Financial Reporting Standards (IFRS) recommends three methods for the calculation of depreciation. They are the straight line, the reducing balance and the units of production method.

4.3.1.1 Reducing Balance Method or Diminishing Balance Method

In this method, a fixed percentage is written off the reducing balance of the asset account each year after a fixed percentage has been written off the first year cost of the asset.

Reducing balance method can also be referred to as a diminishing balance method.

Illustration 1

If a machine is bought for $20,000 and depreciation is to be charged at 20 per cent, the calculations for the first three years would be as follows:

Solution:

Reducing balance method

		$
Cost		20,000
Less first year depreciation	(20% × 20,000)	-4,000
		16,000
Second year depreciation	(20% × 16,000)	-3,200
		12,800
Third year depreciation	(20% ×12,800)	-2,560
Cost not yet apportioned at end of year 3		10,240

4.3.1.2 Straight Line Method

Under the straight line method of depreciation, the cost of acquisition of the asset should be identified. The number of years in which the asset will be put to use should also be identified. The cost is then divided by the number of years. The result is the depreciation charged for each year.

Illustration 1

Machinery was purchased for $50,000 and we estimate that we will put it to use for 6 years and thereafter sold it for $3,500. What is the depreciation charged for each year?

Solution:

Depreciation $= \underline{$50,000 - $3,500}$

$$= \$7,750$$

On the other hand, if we believed that after 6years, the asset will not have a residual value, the charge for depreciation will be:

$$= \frac{\$50,000 - 0}{6}$$

$$= \$8,333.33$$

4.3.1.3 Units of Production Depreciation Methods

The units of production depreciation method is the most accurate and appropriate method of calculating depreciation where the extent and amount of depreciation is determined by the usage of an asset during production.

Its use is limited to those assets for which some estimate of production can be attached, but it is a particular choice of those who use activity-based costing systems because it closely relates asset cost to actual activity.

To calculate it, estimate the total amount of expected units of production that can be produced by the asset. The following are the steps to be taken in calculating it:

Step1

Divide the cost of the assets after residual value (cost – residual value) by the expected total units of production to arrive at depreciation per unit.

Step 2

Multiply the depreciation per unit by the total units of production in a particular accounting period to arrive at the depreciation for the period.

ILLUSTRATION 1

A machine, at an oil company, is assembled at a cost of $700,000. It is expected to be used in the extraction of 2 million barrels of oil, which results in an anticipated depreciation rate of $0.35 per barrel. During the first month, 47,000 barrels of oil are extracted.

What is the depreciation for the period?

SOLUTION:

The depreciation for the month:

= Depreciation per unit of production × total production for the Period

= $0.35 × 47,000 barrels

= $16,450

This calculation also can be used with service hours as its basis rather than units of production. When used in this manner, the method can be applied to a larger number of assets for which production volumes would not be otherwise available.

4.4 Double Entry Records for Depreciation

Recording depreciation involves maintaining each non-current asset at its historical cost. Another ledger account where the depreciation to date is recorded is also kept. This account where depreciation to date is kept is called accumulated provision for depreciation account or accumulated depreciation account.

4.4.1 Double Entry Book-keeping for depreciation:

Debit the statement of comprehensive income (profit and loss account)

Credit the accumulated provision for depreciation account

Example 1

A business has a financial year end of December 31. A computer was bought for $4,000 on January 1,2008. It is to be depreciated at the rate of 20 percent per annum using the reducing balance method. Record the depreciation on double entry bookkeeping.

Solution:

Calculation of depreciation using reducing balance method

		$
Cost as at Jan. 1,2008		4,000
Depreciation, Dec.31, 2008	20% x 4,000	-800
Balance as Jan. 1,2009		3,200
Depreciation, Dec.31, 2009	20% x 3,200	-640
Balance as Jan. 1,2010		2,560
Depreciation, Dec.31, 2010	20% x 2,560	-512
Balance as at Jan. , 2011		2,048

Computer Accounts

_____

2008		$	
Jan. 1	Cash	4,000	

Accumulated Provision for depreciation A/C

2008			$	2008			$
Dec.31	Balance c/d		800	Dec.31	P&L		800
2009				2009			
					Balance		
				Jan. 1	b/d		800
Dec.31	Balance c/d		1,440	Dec.31	P&L		640
			1,440				1,440
2010				2010			
					Balance		
Dec.31	Balance c/d		1,952	Jan. 1	b/d		1,440
				Dec.31	P&L		512
			1,952				1,952
				2011			
					Balance		
				Jan. 1	b/d		1,952

NOTE:

P&L means profit and loss accounts

Statement of Comprehensive Income
(Profit & Loss Accounts)

2008		$
Dec. 31	Acc. Prov. for depreciation	800

2009

Dec. 31 Acc. Prov. for depreciation   640

2010

Dec. 31 Acc. Prov. for depreciation   512

Statements of financial position (extracts)

As at Dec. 31,
2008 $ $
Computer at cost   4,000
Accumulated
Depreciation.   -800
                                                    3,200

As at Dec. 31,
2009
Computer at cost   4,000
Accumulated
Depreciation.   -1,440
                                                    2,560

As Dec. 31, 2010
Computer at cost   4,000
Accumulated
Depreciation.   -1,952
                                                    2,048

4.5 The disposal of a Non-Current Asset

When a non-current asset is sold, we need to remove it from the ledger accounts. This can be done in the following ways:

a) The cost of the asset sold has to be removed from the asset accounts

b) The accumulated depreciation of the asset sold has to be taken out of the accumulated provision for depreciation accounts

c) The profit or loss on the asset sold has to be determined.

Accounting Entries needed are as follows:

The following entries are needed in the sale of a non-current asset:

1. Transfer the cost of the asset sold to an asset disposal account:
Debit asset disposal account
Credit asset account

2. Transfer the depreciation already charged to asset disposal accounts:
Debit accumulated provision for depreciation account
Credit asset disposal account

3. For the amount received from disposal:
Debit bank or cash account
Credit asset disposal account

3. Transfer the difference (i.e. the amount required to balance the asset disposal account) to the statement of comprehensive income (profit and loss account)

a) If the asset disposal account shows a difference on the debit side (profit):
Debit asset disposal account
Credit profit and loss account

b) If the asset disposal account shows a difference on the credit side (loss):
Debit profit and loss account
Credit asset disposals account

ILLUSTRATION 1

Equipment costing $120,000 was bought on 1st January 2001.
Depreciation was provided at 20% annually on straight line method.
It was sold on 30th June, 2004 for $31,500.

You are required to calculate:

a) its accumulated depreciation at the time of sales

b) profit or loss in the year of sales

c) the net book value of the asset at the time of sale

Solution:

a) $3.5 \times 20\% \times \$120,000 = \$84,000$

b)
Equipment Disposal Accounts

	$		$
Cost	120,000	Acc. Depn.	84,000
		Cash	31,500
		P&L	4,500
	120,000		120,000

Loss was $4,500 in the year of sales.

		$
c)	Cost	120,000
	Accumulated depreciation	(84,000)
	Net Book Value	36,000

ILLUSTRATION 2

The table below shows information concerning machinery imported from abroad.

	$
Purchase price of machinery	120,000
Import duty	11,000
Installation cost	5,500
Annual maintenance cost	1,400
Estimated useful life 5years	
Estimated scrap value	6,000

a. What is the total acquisition cost of the equipment?

b. If a straight line method is used, what is the annual depreciation charged?

Solution:

a.

	$
Purchase price of machinery	120,000
Import duty	11,000
Installation cost	5,500
	136,500

b. $\dfrac{136,500 - 6,000}{5} = \$26,100$

4.6 Changes of Depreciation Method

It is possible to make a change in the calculation of depreciation. The change should not be frequent. Where a change to the depreciation is material, the effect of the change on the reported figure should be stated as a note to the financial statement in the year of the change.

4.7 Impairment of Assets

According to IAS 36, impairment of assets ensures that assets are not carried in the statement of financial position at more than their recoverable amount (i.e the higher of fair value less cost of disposal and the value in use)

IAS 36 applies to the following assets:

1) Land
2) Buildings
3) Machinery and equipment
4) Investment property carried at cost
5) Intangible assets
6) Goodwill
7) Investments in subsidiary, associates and joint venture carried at cost
8) Assets carried at revalued under IAS 16 and IAS 38

IAS 36 does not apply to the following assets

1) Inventories
2) Assets arising from construction contracts
3) Deferred tax assets
4) Assets arising from employees benefits
5) Investment property carried at fair value
6) Agricultural assets carried at fair value
7) Financial assets
8) Insurance contracts assets
9) Non-current asset held for sales

Key definitions are as follows:

4.7.1 Impairment Loss

Impairment loss is the amount by which the carrying amount of an asset in the statement of financial position is higher than the recoverable value of the asset.

4.7.2 Carrying amount

Carrying amount is the amount at which an asset is carried in the statement of financial position after deducting accumulated depreciation.

4.7.3 Recoverable amount

Recoverable amount is the higher of an asset fair value less cost of its disposal and its value in use.

4.7.4 Fair Value

Fair value is the price that would be received to sell an asset or paid to transfer a liability in orderly transactions between market participants at the measurement date.

4.7.5 Value in Use

Value in use is the present value of the future cash flow expected to be derived from an asset or cash-generating unit.

4.7.6 Cash Generating Unit

Cash generating unit is a small group of identifiable assets from which cash inflow is expected.

4.7.7 How do we find out that there is impairment?

Every company shall watch out for external and internal indicators of a possible impairment.

4.7.7.1 External indicators are significant decline in market value, significant adverse changes in technological, market, economic or legal environment, increase in market interest rates or rates of return, and carrying amount of company's net assets exceeds market capitalization.

4.7.7.2 Internal indicators are obsolescence or physical damage, internal evidence available that asset's performance will be worse than expected, significant adverse changes to company including plans to discontinue or restructure an operation using the asset or to dispose of it earlier than planned.

Therefore, if the company finds any of these indicators, it should determine asset's recoverable amount and find out whether there is impairment.

The recoverable amounts of the following types of intangible assets are measured annually whether or not there is an indication of impairment of assets:

An intangible asset with an indefinite useful life

An intangible asset not yet available for use

Goodwill acquired in a business combination

Case Study 1

Jevta Ltd. has a machinery that amounted to $70,000 after accumulated depreciation as at December 31,2014. It is discovered that there was a decline in the market value of the machinery. The fair value of the asset as at December 31, 2014 was $65,000 and value in use of the asset was $55,000.

You are required to provide answers to the following questions:

1) What is the carrying amount

2) What is the recoverable value

3) Calculate impairment loss

4) Post the information above to journal

5) Record the asset in the statement of financial position

Solutions

1) The carrying amount of the machinery as at December 31 2014 was $70,000.

2) The recoverable value is the higher of the fair value less cost to sale, and the value in use. The fair value ($65,000) is higher than the value in use ($55,000). Therefore, the recoverable value is $65,000.

3)

	$
Recoverable value	65,000
Carrying amount	-70,000
Impairment loss	5,000

4)

Journal Entry

	$	$
Income statement	5,000	
Machinery		5,000

Being the amount recorded for impairment loss

5)

Statement of financial position as at December 31, 2014

	$
Machinery	100,000
Less accumulated depreciation	(30,000)
	70,000
Less impairment loss	(5,000)
	65,000

Note:
We assume that the accumulated depreciation is $30,000.

4.7.8 How to Account for Impairment Loss

There are two models for accounting for impairment losses:

4.7.8.1 Cost Model

Debit: statement of comprehensive income

Credit: Asset account

4.7.8.2 Revaluation Model

Debit: Equity; revaluation surplus

Credit: asset account

Note:

If there is no positive balance figure on revaluation surplus, cost model should be used.

4.7.9 Reversal of Impairment Loss

Where there is an indication that impairment loss might have been decreased, reversal of impairment loss under cost model is always recognized.

Accounting entries for the reversal of impairment loss are as follows:

Debit: Asset accounts

Credit: statement of comprehensive income (P&L); Reversal of impairment loss

4.7.10 Recoverable Value of an Individual Asset and cash Generating Unit

If it is not possible to calculate the recoverable value of an individual asset, then the recoverable amount of the CGU (cash generating unit to which the asset belongs should be calculated. CGU is a small group of identifiable assets that can generate cash inflow for an entity as a continuous use of the assets and are independent of cash flow from other assets.

Any impairment loss calculated for a CGU should be allocated to reduce the carrying amount of the asset in the following order:

- the carrying amount of goodwill should be first reduced then the carrying amount of other assets of the unit should be reduced on a pro rata basis, which is determined by the relative carrying value of each asset; then
- any reductions in the carrying amount of the individual assets should be treated as impairment losses. The carrying amount of any individual asset should not be reduced below the highest of its fair value less cost to sell, its value in use, and zero.
- If this rule is applied then the impairment loss not allocated to the individual asset will be allocated on a pro rata basis to the other assets of the group.

Example
A cash-generating unit has the following net assets:

	$m
Goodwill	60
Property	120
Plant	180
	360

A recoverable amount has been determined and is $270.

Allocate the impairment loss to the net asset of the entity.

Solution:

	Goodwill $m	Property $m	Plant $m	Total $m
Carrying amount	60	120	180	360
Impairment loss	-60	-12	-18	-90
Carrying value after impairment	0	108	162	270

4.8 Revaluation of Fixed Assets (Non-Current Assets)

Revaluation of fixed assets is the process of increasing or decreasing their carrying amount in case of major changes in the market value of the fixed asset.

International Financial Reporting Standards stipulated that fixed assets should be initially recorded at cost, but they allow two models for subsequent accounting for fixed assets, namely cost model and revaluation model.

4.8.1 Cost Model

Under cost model, fixed assets are carried at historical cost less accumulated depreciation and accumulated impairment losses.

ILLUSTRATION 1

Samotex Ltd. purchased a building worth $100,000 on January 1, 2006. The building has a useful life of 10 years and the company uses straight line method of depreciation. What will be the value of the building at December 31, 2008 and accumulated depreciation for the period?

Record the above information in the book of accounts.

SOLUTION:

Step 1

The building will first be recorded at its historical cost.

Journal Entry

	Dr.	Cr.
	$	$
Building	100,000	
Cash		100,000

Step 2

The historical cost of the building will be reduced by the accumulated deprecation and accumulated impairment loss of the building.

Calculation of accumulated depreciation:

$100,000/10 = $10,000$

Annual depreciation = $10,000$

Accumulated depreciation as December 31, 2008:

$3 \times \$10,000 = \$30,000$

The carrying amount is $100,000 minus $30,000 which equals $70,000.

We can see that the building remains at its historical cost and is periodically depreciated with no other upward adjustment to value.

4.8.2 Revaluation Model

Under revaluation model, an asset is initially recorded at its historical cost, but subsequently adjusted for increase in value to account for any appreciation in value.

The only difference between the cost model and the revaluation model is that cost model only allows downward adjustment due to impairment losses, while revaluation model allows both upward and downward adjustment in value of an asset.

ILLUSTRATION 2

Consider the illustration 1 of Samotex Ltd. as stated in case of cost model. Assume on December 31, 2008, the company intends to switch to revaluation model and carries out revaluation exercise which estimates the fair market value of the building to be $90,000 as at December 31, 2008. The carrying amount at the date is $70,000.

a) What is the amount of upward adjustment if there is any?

b) What is the revalued amount of the building?

SOLUTION:

a)

The upward amount:
= $ 90,000 - $70,000
= $20,000

b)
The revalued amount of the building is $90,000 because the carrying amount of $70,000 increased by $20,000.

Journal entry

	Dr.	Cr.
	$	$
Building	20,000	
Revaluation surplus		20,000

Being the amount of the revaluation of asset

Note:

Upward revaluation is not considered as a normal gain and is not recorded in the income statement rather it is directly credited to equity account called revaluation surplus. Revaluation surplus contains all the upward revaluation of company's assets until all those assets are disposed off.

4.9 Depreciation after Revaluation

Depreciation in the periods after revaluation is based on the revalued amount. Under the illustration of Samotex Ltd., depreciation for 2009 shall be the new carrying amount divided by the remaining useful life or $90,000/7 which is equal to $12,857.14.

4.9.1 Reversal of Revaluation

If a revalued asset is subsequently valued down due to impairment, the loss is first written off against any available balance in the revaluation surplus and if the loss is higher than the balance in the revaluation surplus of the same asset, the difference is charged to the income statement as impairment loss.

ILLUSTRATION 3

Assume on December 31, 2010 Samotex Ltd. revalues the building again to find out that the fair value should be $60,000.

Carrying amount as at December 31, 2010 is $90,000 minus 2-year depreciation (2×12,857.14) which amounts to $64,285.72.

The carrying amount exceeds the fair value by ($64,285.72 - $60,000) = $4,285.72. The revaluation surplus should be reduced by $4,285.72. The company is already having $20,000 in the revaluation surplus account meant for the same asset. This $20,000 is sufficient to absorb the impairment loss ($4,285.72) and hence, there is no need to post the impairment loss to an income statement.

Journal Entry

	$	$
Revaluation Surplus	4,285.72	
Building Account		4,285.72

REFERENCES:

Frank Wood (12th edition) Business Accounting

Adelaja, Toye. O. (2015) Basic Financial Accounting

Adelaja, Toye. O. (2015) Accounting for Depreciation and
    Bookkeeping

 www.accountinghour.com

www.ingramcontent.com/pod-product-compliance
Lightning Source LLC
Chambersburg PA
CBHW070515210526
45168CB00021B/2107